A COLLECTION OF NIGHTMARES

EVEN THE MOST EXQUISITE DREAMS TURN DARK

Praises for *A Collection of Nightmares*

"Participating in a Grand Guignol tradition that traces back to Shelley and Poe…there's a simultaneously more poignant and more disturbing undertow moving just beneath these spiny surfaces: the notion that, against terrifying events beyond our control, the compassion we carry with us will be our only line of defence, our last light shining through the kindness we show, all the more precious for how briefly it flashes."—Mike Allen, author of *Hungry Constellations*

"This is a book of breathtaking artistry. In verse that ranges widely in subject matter and metrical form, Christina Sng invariably focuses on just those words and images that evoke terror, otherworldliness, and fantasy. But deep emotional resonance is not absent, and Sng can evoke poignancy and melancholy as effortlessly as she can evoke fear and dread."—S. T. Joshi

"Christina Sng's poetry gives me the same feeling as observing a Kandinsky painting or hearing a Nine Inch Nails song: something immediate, deeply complex and intensely profound. It is, in short, a wonder."—Jason Erik Lundberg, author of *Strange Mammals*

"As I read this collection, I found myself exclaiming aloud, for there were so many I could relate to, and that is rare for me. Herein are poems that bite you by surprise, delight you with the weave of fresh fabric…A goodly number are dark SF story capsules, from alien interventions to surviving on a world ruined by mankind. I could not pick a single favorite. I loved them all."—Marge Simon, Bram Stoker Award® winning poet

"Each of these fifty or so potent poems are actually stunning little stories about terrifying transformations. Each of the tales she tells are chilling, but her poetic and playful approach spins you around in a vortex of exquisite language and a swirling miasma of wildly terrifying imagination until you yourself are transformed... left dizzy and eager for the next time around. A brilliantly twisted collection, sure to turn a number of heads."—Michael Arnzen, Bram Stoker Award-winning author of *Freakcidents* and *The Gorelets Omnibus*

A COLLECTION OF NIGHTMARES

BY CHRISTINA SNG

RAW DOG SCREAMING PRESS

A Collection of Nightmares © 2017 by Christina Sng

Published by Raw Dog Screaming Press
Bowie, MD

All rights reserved.

First Edition

Cover art: Steven Archer
Cover design: Kevin Kusisto
Book design: Kevin Kusisto
Editor: Stephanie M. Wytovich

Printed in the United States of America
ISBN: 978-1-935738-98-5
Library of Congress Control Number: 2017944013

www.rawdogscreaming.com

Also by Christina Sng

Astropoetry

An Assortment of Sky Things

Catku

A Constellation of Songs

Dark Dreams

The Darkside of Eden

This book is dedicated to my children, my Lightbringers.

TABLE OF CONTENTS

Exquisite 10
Seasonal Creatures 12
The Art of Weaving 13
Just as Papa Said 14
The Bone Carver 16
The Path 17
Mirror to the Other Side 18
Resurrection Dreams 19
They Do Not Sleep 21
Crawlspace 23
That Evening 24
Confession 25
Cocoon 26
The Marvel of Flight 27
Dreams of Bone 29
The Skin Carver 31
Bottled Quiescence 32
Snow Tomb 33
Bruises 34
Death of a Thousand Paper Cuts 35
Inside 36
Visitation by Lady Death 37
Fed to Her 38
Succubus 39
A Mosquito's Tale 43
The Atomizer and the Matchbox 44
The Confluence 46
Full Moon in Yellowstone 48
Sleep Takes a Vacation 49
Crimes of Our Youth 50
Ghost Month 52

The Fall 53
Ravenous 56
D-Day 57
Postwar 60
The Journey 61
Ramblings at the End of the World 63
Children in the Apocalypse 64
After the War 67
Daufin 68
The Awakening 71
Underwater 72
The Flood 74
The Dissection 75
The Monolith 77
Twenty Years 79
The World's Edge 82

Flectere si nequeo superos, acheronta movebo.

If I cannot bend the will of Heaven, I shall move Hell.

—Virgil's *Aeneid*

EXQUISITE

You're exquisite.

Stony-white and frozen,
Parched lips curled
In a delicate snarl—
Medusa caught you
Unexpectedly
That day in her town.

Like the snow queen,
You stand tall, beautiful,
A lone figure, still,
In the rage of winter's furor.
Corpuscles flash frozen, all
But oblivious to time's spiral.

Ten millennia later,
You stand proud
In the heart of my garden,
Immune to hail and rain,
The hatred in your eyes
Wilts the flora in your plane.

Yes, you'd inherited that
From her gaze.
Very formidable,
I must admit.
And today,
I offer a gift.

See my enemies before you
Silent on the ground,

A nail in each crown.
Beneath you,
They blacken and shrivel,
Fading into the ground.

Gorelets ooze,
Swirling beneath your feet,
A pink milky pool, seeping
Into your stony flesh.
Corpuscles revived
In an amalgamated alchemic mesh.

And then you take a step.

SEASONAL CREATURES

We swim in the rivers of blood
At summer time when birds of prey
Patrol the skies, picking off
Those foolish enough to trespass.

In autumn, the skies turn crimson
And carnivorous leaves fall, hoping
To catch a final meal before they
Become part of nature's stockpile.

Then winter falls and we bury ourselves
In soil, bellies warm and full with gullets
And blood, tiding us over till springtime
When we rise again from the dust.

THE ART OF WEAVING

Mommy sat daily at her spinning wheel
Weaving reams of human skin
From the dust we slept in.

When she turned a hundred and three,
She taught the craft to me,
Reminding me time and time again

Never to drop a stitch
Or snag the cloth on
The sharp edges of my spiny flesh.

When I mastered
The art at age fifty-three,
Father taught me how

To breathe life into it.

JUST AS PAPA SAID

The mist had cleared
Before daybreak
When I stumbled out of
The graveyard in tears.
I had raised the dead,
Just as Papa said I would.

Behind me
My family followed,
Dead as posts,
Yet they walked,
Curdled flesh and bones,
Following me back home.

I made up fresh beds,
Laid out fresh sheets,
Washed them gently
With lavender and soap,
Then dressed them
In their Sunday clothes.

I lay beside them,
Kissing each slightly
Rotted cheek, waiting
As the mist outside thickened,
And I whispered to it:
"I wish for another miracle."

In the morning, my heart
Stopped beating, just as
The doctor had said.
Come evening, we sat

Quietly by the fireplace
As we always did,

Dead, but together,
Just as Papa said we would.

THE BONE CARVER

Rain masks the soft hammering in the back room.
Bob is at work again. I imagine him bent over
Yet another bone, chipping away
The excess shards to form a human shape.

I wonder who has crossed Bob today.
And then I remember that cruel boy this morning
Who sneered at my old dress and Bob's torn shoes.
That rich boy from the other side of town.

The memory is a wound
Permanent, reopened daily after school.
Different words from different faces.
They don't last long. But the scars linger.

In the back room, Bob is humming a tune,
Something our mother sang, many years past
When she sculpted megaliths out of clay and bone
Before she too was gone.

The hammering finally stops.
Bob places the bone doll into an airtight box
As we patiently wait for the news:
The boy fallen dead, asphyxiated on the spot.

THE PATH

We walk the path alone,
My child and I in this dark night
Where the only light
Emanates from stars we will not
Visit in our lifetime.

There is nothing but thick forest
On either side. It seems we have
Always walked on this path.
The baby tires and I carry her,
Stumbling over cobblestones,

We fall—
But there is nothing
That cannot be healed.
As she bites into her apple later,
She asks, "Why has he gone?"

How do I tell her he has taken
The other path to where
The magic mushrooms grow?
Where the trees are bare
Lending no shade.

He chose a different path, I say.
But she forgets. We walk again,
Hand in hand, down the endless road,
Slightly limping, but flanked
By an abundance of fruit trees.

MIRROR TO THE OTHER SIDE

Through the mirror
I see him, translucent
In the forest,

Tiny form bent
Over a dying fawn,
Bringing it back to life.

"So what do you think of
Our Mirror to the Other Side?"
The saleslady asks.

I nod and smile, never
Taking my eyes off my boy.
"I'll take it."

RESURRECTION DREAMS

My children,
They are not classical,
Merely whimsical
As every child should be.
Eternally young—
The Peter Pan syndrome
We all live in, chasing
The fountain of youth.

My baby sings about
The rats in the palindrome.
It tickles her to say the words.
She lives in nursery rhymes
Where life is fine and
Endings never cold and bloody
Like the ones I write about
Before I sleep.

But these dark things
Rarely manifest in my dreams.
This is an anomaly.
It must be the wrong mix
Of prescription drugs
When fantasy and reality
Amalgamate in my head.
Come morning, I find

My babies on the floor
Curled up in sweet slumber,
Dreaming of candies and Toyland
And magical forests and trees.
There, they will remain,

In their wonderland
Until it is finally safe
For them to leave.

THEY DO NOT SLEEP

They do not sleep
Even when the world
Is lost in dreaming.
They perch on your bedpost,
Watching you slumber
Night after night, vulnerable in dreams.
Sometimes they touch your mind
And seep into your subconscious.
You won't recall it in the morning,
But later you'll notice you have
Developed new irrational fears.

By day, they hide under your bed,
Beneath your floorboards, in your closets,
On the backs of doors.
They peek through your window
When you are not watching.
As you turn, you only see
A dark shadow scuttle swiftly past
But no one is there when you look back,
And the hairs behind your neck
Rise without warning as a dank chill
Clasps itself around your arid heart.

They are everywhere.
Almost omnipresent, shrouded in shadows.
Rarely, very rarely,
You see them, face to face,
Manifested into your reality.

With brazen bloodshot eyes,
They watch you in the dark,

A clawed hand gripping
The edge of your door as
It eases itself into your silent
Night sanctuary, invading
As you flee into the adjoining
Bathroom, only to find
You have locked yourself
In with it, staring back
In the mirror.
You cannot escape it.

CRAWLSPACE

In the crawlspace,
She squeezes into
Her old familiar spot.
Her spot
Where the horrors
Of the night
Would never cross her,
Especially not
Twenty years later
When she needs to flee
The horrors of humanity
Taunting, teasing, drawing her
To the edge of the precipice,
The beating wind cooing at her
To scream,
Scream
As they cut and crack
Her thin crystal mind
Into daily slices,
Their pound of flesh
To consume
Piece by piece
Till the last screaming portion
Is gone. And here,
They'll never find her,
Not with her old demons
Lying here waiting,
To take a bite out of
Her pretty little head.

THAT EVENING

Your head is in my lap,
As it is always, after our nap.

I stroke your soft black hair
And sing you Marlborough Fair.

Why do your dark eyes stare,
My dear headstrong young mare?

Is my singing no longer fine?
Once you thought it to be divine.

Darling, you look pale and tired.
Suitably, after a day of being wired.

My sweet fireball of lumber,
It is time now for your slumber.

Patting your soft sullen face
Lying so angelic on my mother's fine lace,

I rise from the old sunken couch
In my stiff slow lazy crouch,

Letting your head roll from the lace
Into the screaming fireplace.

CONFESSION

You have ripped out
My tongue; I cannot speak.
My hands spoke for me,
But then you ripped them out too.

Your words churn ice
As you speak. Snow drips
From your lips. I weep
Blood, listening to your confession,
Wishing you had
Ripped out my eardrums instead.

COCOON

I'd like to stay in my cocoon
For as long as I can, till
Hunger cripples me and
Expels me from my shell.
My insides have long been
Cut open and slurped up
By some ravenous god,
Leaving me empty—
A hollow girl.

The chill is paralyzing—
You have known that.
Yet you left me drifting
In the sand dunes,
Parched and dried, my skin
Unfolding in the lacerating wind.
When the dusk finally falls,
I rustle softly as I pass you,
Standing proud in the dust.

THE MARVEL OF FLIGHT

She stands perched
On the peak of the tallest building
Arms outstretched
To form a "T" with her body.

She has dreamed of flying
Since she was a child,
Soaring above skyscrapers
Alongside birds of every variety,

Slicing through clouds
Like a leviathan,
Casting an eclipse
Over the dollhouses below.

A plane speeds past.
She freezes, Pan-like
A Tinkerbell pose,
Before its wake sends her

Somersaulting in the air,
A perfect ten.
She takes a bow
Amidst resounding applause.

The marvel of flight
She thinks with a smile,
As she poises
To plunge

Her cancer-stricken body
Into the air.

And soon,
She is flying.

DREAMS OF BONE

I am bone tired and weary.
These calcified white twigs
Thud dully as they collide,

Collapsing
Into an inverted pyramid,
Remnant of an hourglass

Clasped in a small hand,
Tiny as a bird's, eyes
Saucer-wide, blinking.

I stay by the quiet
Oasis in the sands,
The silent waterfall

With clear blue water
I can breathe in.
I devour serenity

In that old cabin
Sitting on the lip of the lake,
Ebbing over crystalline water

As green grass
Unrolls like a lazy carpet
Over the sighing sand.

Trees emerge, triumphant
From the damp
Dew-drenched grass,

Branches outstretched,
Embracing the sun—
Their long lost friend.

I catch the light
On my pale-death skin,
Torched from summer's kiss,

While swirling black holes
Grind craters into my flesh,
Like exhausted match tips

After a brief, fierce burn.
These scorched blooms,
Autumn's red roses

Once plump and succulent;
Green fields of abundance,
Now oases in winter:

The outcasts of the desert;
The ice sculpture in the fire.
And in the sunshine,

I shatter,
Scattering ash and ice
Over the water—

The cradle of life.
The place of new beginnings.
The land of a dreamless sleep.

THE SKIN CARVER

Let me take your pain

And press it into my skin.
It makes runic inscriptions in my flesh
And disappears into my blood.

The darkness is quelled for a time
And I no longer crave the need
To cut and carve.

But unleash me when you must,
When the agonies of the world
Are finally soothed.

I will draw out my blade
And bring them all back
In an ecstatic bloodbath.

BOTTLED QUIESCENCE

If I could fit into the bottle,
I would drown in absinthe, sink
Into its depths and fill my lungs
With its thick liquid, breathing
Like a rat in perfluorocarbon.

In days my eyes would have turned
Into diamonds, carved into facets
By the magnificence of your blade.
Inside me, you'd remain,
The carrier disease, the plague.

The vampiric eternity, stayed
By your only kryptonite,
As I float in quiet oblivion,
Untouched by hunger and war
Until the sun dies

And I am ready once again
To rise.

SNOW TOMB

Petals fall lazily like snow;
Moments freeze-frame in gold.

On a path painted with blood,
He follows the dark twisted road

Carrying his black carving tools,
Tears falling to the ground

Like sodden old breadcrumbs
Marking his way from her,

Lying in the womb of the cold,
Indulgently carved out in stone.

As life ebbs gently from her throat,
She smiles and sighs in quiet repose.

BRUISES

Under the shroud
Lie the blue bruises
Piled on top of each other
Like boxes in a clutter.
There just isn't enough space
On her thin pallid face.

They crowd about,
Comparing shades,
Who'd been harder hit
And who'd been just a graze.

The day comes
When they become
A single purple mass,
The result of a hand's
Unrepentant rage.

That same day
She picks up the axe
And hacks off
Both his arms and his legs.

His face remains unscathed.
She wants him to watch
Her quick hands
With the carving knife
And be amazed.

DEATH OF A THOUSAND PAPER CUTS

The first,
A delicate kiss,
Then the fluttering
Of an eyelash
Against
The contours of your skin.
Ribbons open gaily,
Like eyes
Wide in surprise,
Then like streams
They gush,
A thousand dams
Unleashed in
Synchronized coincidence.

I've gone through
Every page
Of the encyclopedias,
Every tome.
You read
Like a map,
Journeys criss-crossed
Across the dunes
Dripping
Cherry-red. I have
Covered
Every distinguishing feature
With my savage muse.

INSIDE

I'd like to walk awhile
Inside your skin, have
Your blood swim through
The rivers of mine,
Lounge on the couch
Of your twisted mind,
Dive into your obsessions,
Scouring dark tales
From your grapevine.

Inside
Are the secrets and clues,
The patchwork quilt
Of your actions and cues.
I harbor them, these dark souls
Waiting to be healed.
In them is the key
That will cause you to yield.

With time
I will unravel your puzzle,
Unlock the source
Of your dark inclinations,
Tip the scales
Of your volatile mind,
Turn it counterclockwise
And watch you unwind.

VISITATION BY LADY DEATH

Blood-filled icicles
Grow from my neck
Like wet giant fangs
After a kill.

They snap clean
And fall to my feet
Melting into a puddle
Of my lacerated id.

I turn into ether
In this never-never land.
Peter Pan's doppelgänger
In incandescent form.

Like scattered ashes,
I disperse
Into the atmosphere
Of this cold purgatory.

A reluctant soul.
Hollow, hollow girl.

FED TO HER

Your weakness, her sallow skin
Like that of a skinned rat,

Slapped with brown paint
Where pale skin should be.

Her body,
A gassy gray corpse

You retrieved from the sewers
Last night. The rats animated her,

A soulless creature: not sentient
Nor devoid of conscience.

And you fell in love with her,
Pallid and blue. Your heart

Blackened with charcoal,
Stained with splatters

Of my beaten blood
Stirred, and fed to her.

SUCCUBUS

I.

You have risen in several forms.
A speck in someone's eye,
A painful, annoying zit.

The grit stuck
In a cat's paw.
She gnaws to shake you loose.

A cancer
In a loved one's body.
An almost irreversible scar.

Glass, passed off
As diamonds.
Only blind men will buy you.

II.

Ravenous, a barren bat,
You wandered the track
For a tasty snack.

Spied him in my arms,
Beautiful and young.
The cat got your tongue.

Quiet as cancer, you crept into me,
Plucked the berry from
My chest cavity,

Devoured it
With golden frenzy, spitting
The seed back with dark envy.

(My blood, it
Tasted of honey;
Pyre to your black kidney.)

Gravid with blight, you fled
With he, now impotent of sight,
Away into the limpid night.

And I,
Whipped silent screams
Inside my empty shell

Churning the undercurrent
Of the once-placid lake
Sweeping upward, gushing,

A red geyser spitting globules
Of bloody life; where
Volcanic anger burned, revived.

With crimson hands
I inverted my skin, spilled
The contents deep within

Uncovered my lacerated heart.
It was carved
With your teeth marks.

And I cut it out,
Threw it in the fire.
I would grow another.

III.

Dear pinched pustule,
The stars have realigned;
Fortunes turned, redesigned.

The seasons have moved on,
Shedding their hides,
Leaving you far behind.

In your sleep
You dream of a death
Of a million bites;

A pawnshop
Where the owner
Shatters you on sight.

Peddling your wares
On a frigid
Winter's night;

Being shot and stabbed
In the cross-fire of
A gangland fight.

O, the berry has grown
Into your eye, its tendrils
Rendering you purblind.

Unfurled rind,
You begin to unwind.
The clockwork of your mind

Turns orange and hard,
Like the malignant tumor
In your blood,

Chafing all others.
She who birthed you
Cowers in disgust

Inward, and at you.
She'd known from the start,
But she let you, Black Death,

Pariah of the land,
You were poisoned
By your own hand.

A MOSQUITO'S TALE

You stare at your dead squashed body,
And at me, to see if I am sorry.
But I flick you off my book,
And continue with my story.

THE ATOMIZER AND THE MATCHBOX

Tired of being constantly touched,
Felicette Méchant invented
The Atomizer. It shrunk
The atoms of anyone
Who touched her
Without her
Permission,
Packaged
Into a
Tiny
Spray
Bottle.
Soon she
Could keep
All her enemies
In a matchbox, each one
Carefully taped under a tiny
Microscope. She named the box
Her Happy Matchbox and marketed it
With the Atomizer. The world population
Shrunk exponentially as more errant folk
Ended up Atomized and unceremoniously
Taped into Felicette's Matchboxes,
Ready to be set ablaze whenever
The buyer so desired. That was
The catchphrase. Apart from
A few hardcore ones, most
Were content to display
Their boxes, show off

At parties, and for
The recommended
Daily gloat,
Scaring
The tiny folk
With a giant eye
Blinking repeatedly
In their tiny paper sky.

Felicette Méchant received
The Nobel Peace Prize in 2025
From the United Nations Board
For achieving the impossible:

Peace on Earth, at a price, of course.

THE CONFLUENCE

The lizards are hiding again.
They see the veil falling.
The cats crawl carefully
Away from the basement.

We feel nothing;
Our senses numb, instincts
Dulled from our eyes
Constantly fixed on screens.

Below, the maw smiles,
Opening a conduit
Between the Universe
And the fiery land of Hell.

Predatory creatures
Begin creeping up
The claustrophobic chasm.
It is tenuous as thread.

At the confluence,
They hesitate. Our air ignites
The incendiary brutes,
The first few exploding.

Putrid gas fills the cellar
Like a helium balloon,
The scent of death thick
As gravid rain clouds.

They become fractious,
Turning on each other,
Their triumphant return
Thwarted by a technicality:

Earth's air composition
Has changed drastically
Since they last visited,
Back when it was on fire.

I plug in the hair dryer
After my shower, forgetting
The rental's defective wiring.
It short-circuits the house,

Sending an enormous bolt
Of electricity to blast
The confluence shut. And then,
Life goes on as it was.

FULL MOON IN YELLOWSTONE

Full moon
In Yellowstone—
The Jackalopes return.

I sit on the porch
In Grandma's rocking chair,
Shotgun across my chest,

Thor, my gray tabby
By my side, ears perched,
Discomforted.

I hear the wolves howl.
The mountains rattle
As the Jackalopes feast.

Come morning,
The rangers ask, where
Have all the wolves gone?

I shrug and swig
My last whiskey shot,
As I bolt my door

And head to the attic,
Waiting
For the long night to start.

SLEEP TAKES A VACATION

Sleep has gone on vacation,
Left us bleary-eyed and confused.
Our hands shake at the popping
Of excessive sleeping pills which
Have now dwindled to no effect.

We've become a city of wide-eyed
Shell-shocked zombies, wandering
Lost when night's curtain falls.
By day, the silence disconcerts.
The city stalls.

Sleep returns one fine sunny day,
Fresh from her rest and smiling.
The city falls to slumber immediately
In the midst of chaos and destruction.
Sleep surveys the wreckage and

The blood-smeared pavements,
Shakes her head at the frozen stares
Beyond her touch. As always,
After a long vacation, she has
A ton of work to catch up on.

CRIMES OF OUR YOUTH

The crimes of our youth
Return to haunt us by day
In the faceless masses
We've slaughtered;

Shrouded intent masked
Behind those tight polite smiles,
Moon faces beaming, their
Pearly whites catching the light.

By night, they are shadows,
Specters peering out of the nooks
We unknowingly glance at.
The abyss never rests.

For once
I'd like to breathe
Without forever losing
Half a beat in distress.

They follow us around
To every street and
Every town. The unexplained
Sounds in the ceiling,

Strange high-pitched shrieks
When the clock strikes twelve.
The broken mirror on the wall,
And the red-eyed man

Standing there watching,
Then gone, as we blink,
And venture to check, but
There's no one there at all.

Tomorrow morning
I'll take a shovel. Unearth
The three dozen we'd mauled,
And rest them on holy ground.

GHOST MONTH

August rain falls lightly
On the summer-scorched soil.

The ghost month is taking its toll,
Spirits abound a thousandfold.

They swirl like tendrils unfurled
In a crack-ridden tsunami ride

And feast on the offerings
Laid on the ground, reliving

Their death stories
In mists of clouds.

THE FALL

It began with the great oak
Felled for a new condominium complex.

The neighboring foliage watched fearfully
Worried they would be next.

Quietly they sent urgent pleas
Through airborne spores

Carrying the message
That the humans must be stopped.

To the ends of the Earth
They flew

And the message, passed from spore
To spore, gradually became one of war.

*

Wall-crept ivy
Learnt to process chlorophyll

At an Olympic rate,
Leeching from the grass below

Till the ground turned
Jaundiced and fallow.

At the brink of dawn
The ivy choked to death

All those who drew near,
Creating a green mural

Of death throes, before
Stretching its arms

To move next door.

*

In the cities,
Leaves from overhanging trees

Fell prematurely in summer,
Raining manufactured poison

Onto unsuspecting people
Who happened to walk by.

The infectious rash spread,
Causing many to go mad,

Suicidal from the agony
Of their shredded arms and hands.

*

In the country,
Orchards sprung drugged produce.

Their flesh turning acidic
Once they were eaten.

As they fell from broken throats,
The soil became fertile

With more bitter harvests,
Sprouting plants and trees

Borne from the mix
Of human blood and poisoned flesh.

*

Civilization collapsed.

Without sanity,
Humans could not self-organize.

Those not driven mad
Generally starved to death

Even after feeding on
Their species' numerous corpses.

Finally, when the battlefield
Quietened, and the only sound

Was the woosh of the curious wind,
The ground took into its arms

Its offering—
All that remained.

And as if they never existed,
The human race vanished completely

Without a trace.

RAVENOUS

The fronds reached for the sky,
Grazing the clouds with their leafy arms,
Sipping the mist from Avalon's heaven.

Soon they grew thick as a forest,
Cuddling in swarms, consuming storms
At their moment of birth.

Below, we dehydrate like parchment,
As the forest in the sky grows,
Drowning us under an eternal night.

D-DAY

I prepared them for D-Day
From the time they were born—
The day we had to flee.

The fire began in the horizon,
At 3am one summer night
Beneath the rising blood moon.

It devoured house after house,
Their inhabitants incinerated
Before they could scream.

Soon an orange glow flickered
From under the bedroom door.
Smoke poured in like dry ice,

The scent unmistakable,
Waking me up
From a restless slumber.

I swiftly opened the windows
As Jack sped to the bathroom
To wet three towels.

Ava woke up, her eyes bleary.
I tied a rope around her waist
And lowered her like we practiced.

Smoke began to fill the room,
Looming like an angry fog monster,
Swirling around my son

While he helped me hold the rope.
Ava reached the ground, untied herself
And beckoned us to hurry.

I lowered Jack next.
He gave me the thumbs up
As he reached the ground

And quickly untied the knots,
Mouthing the words,
"Hurry, Mom!"

I hoped the window frame would hold.
Using the rope as a secondary support,
I rappelled down the roof

And leapt off the parapet.
The children were waiting,
Clutching me tight as we hastened

To our car parked on the street.
Houses exploded on both sides of us.
"It has begun," Jack said solemnly.

I nodded, one eye on little Ava
Hugging her favorite stuffed cat whom
She somehow managed to smuggle along.

The spaceship was where we left it,
But we needed to be in our own form
To pilot it.

We hyperventilated
Till our human skin shed,
Our thick corrugated hides shook

And stretched
From years of compression.
Jack grinned, happy to be himself again.

I placed my hoof on the panel
As the ship sighed and started.
We had to hurry.

The Exterminators had found us,
The ones who destroyed our planet.
We were the last of our kind,

And they would not rest
Till every living thing
Was scorched and dead.

Our water-fueled ship achieved lightspeed.
We would find another planet to hide in,
To grow and survive.

By then, the eggs would all be hatched,
And we could finally train an army
To fight back.

Little Ava cradled her stuffed cat
With her twin hooves.
She lay back

And softly meowed to her toy.
One more language learned.
One more planet lost.

POSTWAR

The scent of burnt flesh
Seeps into my pores.
They are burning the corpses.

I venture an open eye,
Scan the war-beaten horizon
Which boasts only

Of charred bodies and corn stalks.
Beside me, a child lies curled,
Holding her cat in her arms.

She looks at me, eyes wide
As I scoop her up and dash across
The barren field into our shelter below.

Safe, she asks for my name,
Exchanges it with hers.
Her cat's name is Perry, she adds,

And her parents are dead.
I ask if she knows what has happened today.
How our people were crushed in their iron fists.

She nods and asks,
The humans have won,
Haven't they? Yes, I say.

And I lead her into the sewers,
Our new home, where she summons Perry
To catch us some prey.

THE JOURNEY

I have walked
Eleven days to find you.
The world has gone to hell
Since the first asteroids fell.
I still shiver with a numbing chill,
Remembering the forty hours I spent
Curled up beside Joe's frozen corpse
In the lift of our apartment building.

The blasts roared like thunder,
Flames shot high as towers.
The sky frowned, a sullen gray.
It would not let sunlight
Through its thick angry shroud.
The fire expired after a while,
Took its last breath, and then
Eternal winter claimed its ground.

Alone, I threaded through
The ruins of our town,
Once upon a time,
Our home, our safe place.
Frost grew like moss
Around my pounding heart
As I saw dead bodies spilled like seeds
Around the charred burial ground.

But I went on,
Knowing where I could find you.
Knowing you'd know what to do.
You were the wise one, the sage.

You'd understand why
I had to leave him cold and alone
In that iron coffin where I
Almost chewed off his arm
Out of hunger but stopped myself
Out of love.

And now I stand before you,
Shaking under the frigid sky.
You clasp your arms around me,
Your voice, like electricity in water
As you ask, "Where is Joe?"
The words are stuck in my throat - I choke.
But you know, weeping
While you stroke my matted fur,
Carrying me back home
To the torn building behind.

RAMBLINGS AT THE END OF THE WORLD

I lurk by the sewer
Waiting for a catch.
Some days I get cockroaches,
Other days I get rats.

One time there were cicadas
Nesting where I sat.
They made a hearty meal.
They tasted just like bat.

The desert heat is like sand.
It crawls under your skin.
Everything is dead,
I wait at Earth's rim.

The world has gone mad
Since the dark sky fell.
Fire engulfed the land,
Work of one nuclear shell.

The cold dead are scattered
In crisp burnt heaps,
Half-buried in sand,
They turn to sleep.

CHILDREN IN THE APOCALYPSE

We feared the baby's cries would kill us all,
But we were wrong. Mara sits happily in
Her baby carrier with nary a sound, but
A small squeak when she is hungry or wet.

Quickly satiated with a nurse and a change,
She never did draw our enemies as we thought,
Since the virus was released and
People turned into rabid cannibals.

Routine culling of the weak, they call it.
We, the outsiders, the ones beyond the wall,
Are anathema to the elite. We were once
Scientists, writers, teachers, and artists,

All of us slowly edged out of the city and
Flung into the wastelands, where we are bait
For their experimental soldiers, the latest—
Zombies, we have to call them. Expendable,

Reproducible, perfectly controlled,
With the ability to successfully recruit
While on mission. Once bitten, we turn
In an hour, and then we fight for them.

Now we flee for the mountains, our home
No longer safe. The wastelands are overrun
With zombies, new ones made every day.
There will soon be nowhere to hide.

Mara gurgles as I tighten the carrier
Around me. I kiss my son Simon's sweet
Baby cheeks as I tell him to hold on tight.
He wedges his hands between Mara and I.

Only 4, but braver than any adult I've met.
Last night he put an axe in the face
Of a zombie that surprised me.
"Dad is dead," he said.

"It is my turn to protect you and Mara.
We must leave this place before everyone
Is turned. Please Mom, we must go. Now."
I wept for the loss of his childhood.

But he feels no such loss. Wisdom and
Responsibility have taken over. These times
Dictate it. There are no more safe zones.
He is right. It is time to go.

Quietly, we pack our supplies,
Tie them securely to my old scrambler,
Tommy Ray. I kickstart the bike.
The noise is deafening,

Echoing through the dead alleys
And silent streets.
The zombies stir and run.
But we are faster, for once.

Tommy Ray darts forward
And onto the dusty road.
He speeds up to 100 miles an hour.
In the side mirror,

I see the zombies recede.
Mara keeps watch over my shoulder.
Simon and I look ahead
To the looming green mountains.

AFTER THE WAR

Greed drives through
Our war-torn country
In a shiny red Cadillac.
The tires are greased

With live roadkill, lining
The streets with fresh meat.
Bodies litter the broken towns
As virgin white snow once did.

The few who remain
Divide loyalties,
And slay all those
In their way.

The world swings upside down
As Wonderland turns to hell.
Alice transforms
Into the Wicked Witch

To drive the punters
From her cell.
Humpty kills the king's men
With her fall, rules the state

From her red brick wall.
Clamping an iron fist,
She restores order
From radiated mist.

DAUFIN

The sea turned green
The night I was born.
It tasted of rotted fronds
And dead anemones.
My first memory.

Yet I grew, gargantuan
Even for my family.
And oh, they feared me.
Called me cursed.
Drove me from the clan,

Slaughtered my mother
For defending me.
So I tore them to shreds,
Ribbons in the sea.
Now there is only me.

I followed the tides
From one end of our world
To the other,
Where the waters
Were gentler, sweeter

But the bitter tang,
That copper scent
Always remained.
A reminder
Of my old home.

And then I grew up
Made offspring of my own.
Miniature me's.
I adored them all.
Now we were three.

I took them back
To where I was born,
Where the new prey
Tasted of home.
A flood of memories flashed:

A shiny tube
From the surface
Drifting down
To the seabed,
Bleeding moss-colored liquid

Where my clan nested
Throughout my mother's
Pregnancy, pumping her belly
Full of poison, killing all
Her offspring but me.

Born ravenous with hunger,
I devoured those tiny worms
Circling the tube, screaming,
"Daufin, daufin!"
Until the pain went away.

In time,
My offspring grew,
Larger than me,
Made another few.
And again the younglings grew.

Now I watch them beach,
Stretch their flippers,
Form them into a foot,
Step onto sand.
They are on land.

I watch from the sea.
A shrill symphony
Resounds through me.
They have found the worm nest.
It is time to feed.

THE AWAKENING

In the heart of the caldera
They hatch under the blazing sun,
Incubated for a billion years
Under salted frost that was once an ocean.

Flailing like saplings,
They reach for the sky
Toward the cotton clouds
That descend, looming

Over their long-awaited offspring.
Gently, the breeze carries
The infants across the dead valley,
Toward the bustling city

Which they envelop
Street by street, consuming
Everything within their reach.
Soon they are as large

As their ancient parents, and
Leaving the dead city behind,
As a single dark cloud,
They cross to the next continent.

UNDERWATER

We'd moved under the sea.
With the dispersion of the ozone layer,
The rising tides, and the lack of funding
For the space-rehabilitation program,
All we had was undersea-faring technology
Out of the twenty-second century.

Of course, we couldn't all go.
Those left behind plunged underwater
In desperation, their skins charred
And bloated when they drowned
And became fish food.
That was where it began, the survivors said,
In resigned retrospection.

Marine life near the surface
Died from excessive UV exposure.
Soon only the deep sea creatures endured,
Leaving us, residing just beside them,
Their only prey. We never realized
How large they were this deep under.
They were too fast, too well-camouflaged
For our mechanical probes to detect.

Now I've finished saving our logs
On various mediums.
It is hopeful that someday,
Surface survivors, perhaps from
The coldlands, may find them and
Decode them, carry on our human heritage.

The pounding of our habitat continues.
An eye immensely larger than my porthole
Peers at me from a distance away.
I shut it quickly.
It is only a matter of time
Before they open this can.
And when they do, let's see
If they will be fast enough to catch us
Before we implode.

THE FLOOD

Blood rain screams to the ground
In a mad torrent of rage,
Stirring up a thick muddy flood,
As it clouds the world with sludge.

Bridges and buildings
Are swept under its fold,
A titanic undercurrent
Churning sand into liquid gold.

Earth's denizens flee
Like ants in a puddle
Under the watchful eye
Of a curious god.

The moon blinks impassively
With its single-pearled eye
As it turns to sleep, indifferent
To the blazing red sky.

THE DISSECTION

We won the war
Against the invaders.
By accident, of course.

Now several million carcasses
Of the mile-long alien jellyfish
Lie scattered all over the world.

Scientists flocked to study them,
Setting up camps around
The perimeter of the creatures' bodies.

We discovered their luminous shells
Could turn hard as titanium
With exposure to enough radiation.

Another specimen slammed shut
Like a clam, air tight.
A vacuum seal.

They'd evolved, reengineered
Their own bodies as spaceships,
Immune to radiation.

We should have expected
Weaponry as well.
The first cut into their flesh

With the diamond drill
Released a putrid gas,
Lulling us all to sleep

While converting
Earth's air
To pure methane.

The remainder of us,
Deep underground in bunkers
Watched as the next fleet descended,

Retrieving the bodies of the Trojans,
Who had already terraformed our Earth
Into their own.

THE MONOLITH

And there we saw it,
Looming on the horizon,
Black against granite black:
A colossal tower rising.

It hovered statue-like, mid-air
And then a shrill resonance
Thundered through Earth
Imploding water into gas.

Inside and out we geysered,
Rivulets of death splattered
Across our blue planet, splotches
Of red against the green and brown.

The crimson seas raged with the
Blood of innocents. Millions of years
Of evolution—life's masterpiece—
Washed away in the snow.

Those who burrowed, survived.
Underground in lead boxes,
We lived on stale food and filtered air.
Never again to touch sunshine,

Not with our bare skin,
Nor feel the dew
On soft green grass
Underfoot at dawn.

The years passed
And the survivors passed.
This is not life,
Whispered the last

Climbing out of her metal shell,
Dead children in her arms.
She stood on charred land,
Thick fumes choking her lungs.

As she fell, the monolith
Slipped quietly back into the sky.
She turned her face towards it
And softly asked, "Why?"

Then
As quiet as the sunrise,
I closed my eyes,
And faded into the light.

TWENTY YEARS

The hovercraft loomed,
A silent sentinel watching
Over me and my little ones,
Waiting to take us
To a new home,

A new life.
Away from our dying planet,
Where the rising seas
Have washed away the cities,
Drowning all life and humanity.

The promise was
A blue-green planet
Twenty light years away.
The caveat: we had to
Leave our old behind.

I held my mother's hand,
Wrinkled and dry, now
Damp with tears
Free-falling from her face.
And Papa

Standing beside her,
Our rock, full of emotion
He would never show
But a glisten in his eyes,
A trick of the light.

She grazed my cheek
With the soft back of her hand,
Like she did when I was little.
Dear girl, we are eighty.
We have lived.

Even if we could go,
We would not live to see
The new world. It would be
Twenty years in a ship.
Death on a ship.

I grew desperate, tears
Blinding. I grasped her hand
Tighter. We could stay.
The planet is a pipe dream.
We might not breathe.

Here, we can fish,
Live in the mountains.
We can find a way.
I would rather twenty years
Here with you

Than eternity in a metal box
Full of empty promises.
Papa's hand fell gently
On my shoulder. Child,
He said. You must think

Of them. His eyes turned
To my children, both
Bright-eyed and happy,
Dancing around their
Grandparents, oblivious

To the agony we felt.
I held his eyes, and saw
Conflict and sadness
And a determination
To do what was right.

As did I.

I nodded to the pilot
Who saluted and left.
I embraced my mother
And father, and held
My children tight.

Together we watched
The hovercraft depart.
Mama said, now we
Have twenty years
Together.

No, I said.
We have forever.

THE WORLD'S EDGE

The seas rose last night,
Washing away cities and continents.

The world perished below us
As we, far from civilization,
Went along our daily lives,
Tending to our small garden
And family of five,
High up in the mountains.

At dusk, the seas whisper to me,
The end of days has come.
But I ignore them.
We live outside of time,
Far beyond society's reach.
It was my choice: my family.

Alice is reading an ancient novel,
Jack playing with a ball of wool,
Ava and Jade are curled up by the window,
Dreaming of prey they'd caught
In their yesteryear while I stand
On the porch watching the world go by.

The seas will reach us in time
Alice says, and we too, will be
Washed away with the world.
But I shake my head and tell her,
There isn't enough water
To drown us, to drive us away.

But then the day comes
When civilization finds us,
Bringing boatloads of survivors
To claim our ground. Alice
And I take our small family
Into one of our old dinghies

And sail off to the world's edge
Where we belong.

PREVIOUSLY PUBLISHED

Aoife's Kiss. "The Monolith." 2012.

Apex Magazine. "The Dissection." 2015.

Black Petals. "A Mosquito's Tale," "Inside," and "Visitation by Lady Death." 2001-02.

ChiZine. "The Bone Carver." 2003.

Dark Animus. "Bottled Quiescence," "Death of a Thousand Paper Cuts," and "Sleep Takes a Vacation." 2003-04.

Devolution Z. "Children in the Apocalypse." 2016.

Electric Velocipede. "Just as Papa Said," "Snow Tomb," "The World's Edge," and "Underwater." 2002-06.

Exquisite Corpuscle. "Exquisite." 2009.

Flesh & Blood. "Seasonal Creatures," "The Art of Weaving," and "They Do Not Sleep." 2002-04.

frission: disconcerting verse. "Confession." 2001.

Ghostlight: The Magazine of Terror. "The Atomizer and the Matchbox." 2016.

Horror Writers Association Poetry Writers Showcase. "The Skin Carver." 2015.

Lunatic Chameleon. "Bruises" and "The Journey." 2002-04.

Mythic Delirium. "Crawlspace," "Dreams of Bone," and "Mirror to the Other Side." 2003-16.

New Myths. "Full Moon in Yellowstone" and "Twenty Years." 2015-16.

Penny Dreadful. "The Fall." 2005.

Penumbric. "Resurrection Dreams," "That Evening," and "The Awakening." 2003-04.

Polu Texni: "D-Day." 2016.

Southern Gothic. "Fed to Her" and "Ramblings at the End of the World." 2001.

Space and Time. "After the War" and "Ghost Month." 2002-07.

*Star*Line.* "The Confluence." 2015.

Tales of the Talisman. "Daufin." 2011.

Tapestry. "The Path." 2001.

The Darkside of Eden. "Succubus." 2002.

The Edge: Tales of Suspense. "Cocoon." 2001.

The Pedestal Magazine. "Postwar." 2001.

Wicked Hollow. "Crimes of Our Youth," "The Flood," "The Marvel of Flight," and "Ravenous." 2002.

AWARDS

"The Path", First Prize, *The Tapestry Poetry Contest*, 2001

"The Marvel of Flight", Honorable Mention, *Year's Best Fantasy and Horror 16*, 2003

"Crimes of Our Youth", Honorable Mention, *Year's Best Fantasy and Horror 16*, 2003

"The Bone Carver", Honorable Mention, *Year's Best Fantasy and Horror 17*, 2004

"Death of a Thousand Paper Cuts", Third Prize, *Dark Animus Award*, 2002-3

"The Art of Weaving", Honorable Mention, *Year's Best Fantasy and Horror 18*, 2005

"Twenty Years", Nomination, *Rhysling Poetry Award (Long Poem)*, 2016

ACKNOWLEDGEMENTS

My deepest thanks and appreciation to my publishers, Jennifer Barnes and John Edward Lawson, and to my editor Stephanie Wytovich, for believing in my work and taking a chance on me.

I am especially grateful to the friends, publishers, editors, and colleagues who have walked with me on my poet's journey. I would not have made it here without them:

Linda Addison, Dawn Albright, Anita Allen, Mike Allen, the late James Baker, Scott T. Barnes, F.J. Bergmann, Shelly Bryant, Susan Burch, Tyree Campbell, Charles Christian, Jennifer Crow, Sandy DeLuca, J Alan Erwine, Jeff Georgeson, Michael H. Hanson, Grace Ho, Jon Hodges, Gerard Houarner, S.T. Joshi, Sandra Kasturi, John Klima, Deborah P Kolodji, Warren Lapine, Shen-Li Lee, Angeline Liu, Jason Erik Lundberg, David C. Kopaska-Merkel, Diane Severson Mori, John Reinhart, Marcy Rockwell, Karen A. Romanko, Teri Santitoro, Marge Simon, Jason Sizemore, Bianca Spriggs, David Lee Summers, Marcie Tentchoff, Scott Urban, Susan Shell Winston, Shannon Connor Winward, Kumie Wise, Bryan Thao Worra, and Frank Wu.

Special thanks to my Mom and Dad for their love and support, and to my late cat Boy, my first light in the long dark.

And finally, thank you to my children for their infinite patience and grace. It has been my greatest joy being their mom.

ABOUT THE AUTHOR

Christina Sng is a poet, writer, and artist. She earned her BA in Criminology and Philosophy from the University of Melbourne and spent most of her career as a web consultant, content producer, UX strategist, and information architect.

Since 2001, Christina's work has appeared in numerous venues worldwide, especially her poetry which garnered many accolades over the years, most notably nominations in the Dwarf Stars and Rhysling Awards, as well as Honorable Mentions in the *Year's Best Fantasy and Horror*.

Her recent collections include *A Constellation of Songs*, *Astropoetry*, and *Catku*. *An Assortment of Sky Things*, her chapbook of space poems, was nominated for the 2017 Elgin Award. *A Collection of Nightmares* is her first full-length book of dark poetry.

www.ingramcontent.com/pod-product-compliance
Lightning Source LLC
Chambersburg PA
CBHW032024040426
42448CB00006B/713